THE SONG EVERLASTING
✝

MINISTRY • HUMILITY • VICTORY

A SACRED CANTATA BASED ON EARLY AMERICAN SONGS

By Joseph M. Martin

Orchestration by Brant Adams
Appalachian Consort by Stan Pethel

CONTENTS

Performance Time: Approximately 45 minutes

① This symbol indicates a track number on the StudioTrax CD (Accompaniment Only).

Harold Flammer
MUSIC

A DIVISION OF SHAWNEE PRESS, INC.
EXCLUSIVELY DISTRIBUTED BY HAL LEONARD CORPORATION

Visit Shawnee Press Online at
www.shawneepress.com

FOREWORD

Music has always been a strong metaphor to teach lessons about life and faith. The chanting of psalms was a foundational part of Hebrew worship. The Apostle Paul used song illustratively as he encouraged the early church to live in harmony. From the upper room, distant tones of our Savior's voice could be heard as He and His friends sang into the shadows and found their song in the night.

Music reaches deep into our hearts and calls us to reflection. It surrounds us with sound and invites our spirits to soar in celebration. When shared with sincerity, song transcends the walls that separate us and builds bridges of understanding among all people. On the wings of music, we can express the deepest emotions of our lives and explore the victories and mysteries of our faith.

In this cantata I have incorporated hymns, spirituals and folksongs, and intersected these musical moments with the story of Christ's ministry among us. This exalted theme reverberates through the ages in echoes of assurance and its resounding glory is a magnificent never-ending alleluia that awakens in the believer the voice of praise.

It is that same assurance that inspired the early poet to write:

...no storm can shake my inmost calm while to this Hope I'm clinging. Since Christ is Lord of heaven and earth, how can I keep from singing?

JOSEPH M. MARTIN

PROGRAM NOTES

The Song Everlasting is divided into three separate suites of anthems. These sections, entitled Ministry, Humility and Victory, can be performed individually during Lent, Holy Week or Eastertide respectively, or as a larger work in its entirety. In addition to the nine anthems, there are optional congregational hymns included in the back of the choral book for those churches wishing to involve their entire fellowship in the worship experience. I have provided narration to introduce these moments should you choose to use them. There is one hymn at the conclusion of each suite to bring that section to completion and to act as a congregational response to the spiritual concepts delivered by the anthems.

The final number, "The Sure Foundation," can be considered optional if you prefer to perform this cantata in conjunction with your Easter celebrations. In that scenario, "Christ is Risen" can act as the final anthem of the work, and the optional hymn response may be included afterwards, as a final "going forth" congregational moment. Another option would be for the work to simply end with "Christ is Risen" and its festive alleluias.

SCRIPTURE OF PREPARATION
(may be read or comtemplated silently)

Sing People of Zion; shout aloud, children of God. Be glad and rejoice with all of your heart. The Lord, the King of Israel, is with you; never again will you fear any harm. He will take great delight in you; in His love He will forgive you and rejoice over you with singing.
(Zephaniah 3:14-17)

THE WONDROUS STORY

Words by
FRANCIS H. ROWLEY (1854-1952) alt.
PHILIP P. BLISS (1838-1876) alt.

Tune: **HOLY MANNA**
American Folk Hymn
Arranged by
JOSEPH M. MARTIN (BMI)

With rustic energy (♩ = ca. 124)

SOPRANO

ALTO

mf unis.

* I will___ sing the

won - drous sto - ry of the Christ who died for

me;

TENOR

mf unis.

BASS

how He left His home in glo - ry

for the cross of Cal - va - ry.

I was lost, but Je-sus__ found me, found the sheep that went a-stray; threw His__ lov-ing arms a-round__ me;__ drew me__ back in-to His way.

led.

* I will sing of my Re - deem - er and His bound - less love to me.

I will sing of my Re - deem - er and His bound - less

He from death to life hath brought me, Son of God with

love to me. He from death to life, Son of God with

* Words: Philip P. Bliss, 1838-1876, alt.

THE SONG EVERLASTING - SATB

I. MINISTRY

NARRATOR:

The Song began quietly at first. The One who sang the universe into being reached out from a manger bed seeking the comfort of His mother's arms. The newborn's soft cries mingled with Mary's gentle lullaby and there, amid a consort of beasts, the music of grace began to sound.

Soon the Child grew strong and His wisdom increased. The glory of the Lord was upon Him and He began to testify in the temple. His message was older than time itself – an ancient theme that had been echoed for centuries by the prophets; but now the One called Jesus was sharing a new song.

The people began to be amazed at what they heard, and they longed to fill their empty hearts with the beauty of His song of life. They had long-groped in darkness, surrounded by the noise of a hopeless world desperately searching for a home and a purpose. And so, seeing the people longing for a new alleluia… Jesus had compassion and began to teach them!

SONGS OF THE WAYFARER

Tunes:
MOTHERLESS CHILD
and **WAYFARIN' STRANGER**
Arranged by
JOSEPH M. MARTIN (BMI)

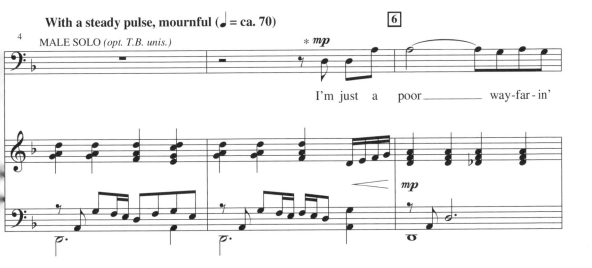

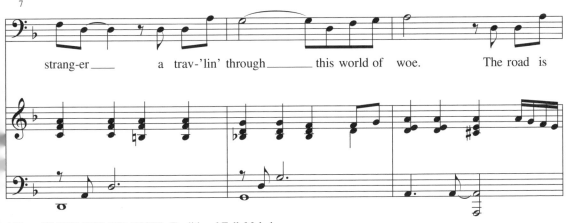

* Tune: WAYFARIN' STRANGER, Traditional Folk Melody
Words: Traditional Folk, alt.

lead_____ me from this dark-ness and bring me

SOPRANO / ALTO (tutti)

Oo

to_____ the Prom-ised Land.

Oo_____ the Prom-ised Land.

FEMALE SOLO (opt. S.A. unis.)

Some - times I feel like I'm al - most gone.____

* Tune: MOTHERLESS CHILD, Traditional Spiritual
Words: Traditional Spiritual, alt.

THE SONG EVERLASTING - SATB

Some-times I feel like I'm al - most gone.___

through_____ this world of woe. The road is

Ah_____ Al - most gone!

Some-times I feel like I'm al - most gone;___ a

filled_____ with toil and dan - ger,___ a

Ah_____ Al - most gone; a

NARRATOR:

Jesus began to share the good news of the kingdom of God. He reached out to all who were seeking and brought peace to those who were troubled and burdened. He began to do marvelous works among the people who followed Him. At a wedding celebration He turned water into wine. Later, a royal official pleaded with Him to save his son, and Jesus healed him. At the city fountain, a paralyzed man leaped to his feet rejoicing at the sound of Jesus' healing words. As He journeyed throughout Judea, the music of His message began to crescendo with purpose. His tender voice fell on the hearts of the weary like a canticle of hope, and to all who would listen, He sang, "Come unto me, and I will give you rest."

for Phoebe Wendler, in celebration of her retirement after 60 years as
Music Director of Faith Evangelical Lutheran Church, Saginaw, MI

COME UNTO ME

Words by
JOSEPH M. MARTIN (BMI)

Tune: **RESIGNATION**
Southern Harmony, 1835
Arranged by
JOSEPH M. MARTIN (BMI)

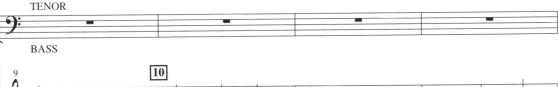

O__ come to__ me, a - bide with__

Come lay your bur - dens at my feet. Your strength I will re - new.

O come to me, con -

you will find new life.

Come and find new life. Come

Learn from me, come serve with me.

learn from me, come serve with me and

Fill the earth with light. Leave

fill the earth with light.

28

far be - hind your path of sin and run to my em - brace. My lov - ing arms will keep you safe.

(Accompanist may double voices if desired.)

unis.

p

Oo

I'll shel - ter you with grace.

I'll shel - ter you with

grace.

NARRATOR:

From village to village the Teacher went and the music of grace began to resound throughout the land. The people gathered to Jesus and their lives were transformed by the sound of His voice. The sick became healthy and the lame began to dance and sing. Soon it seemed as if the whole nation was following the Singer in a great procession of praise and thanksgiving. To many it was clear this was the Promised One whom the prophets had spoken, "The Lord God is in your midst, a Mighty One who will save. He will quiet you by His love. He will exult over you with loud singing."

JOURNEY OF HOPE AND PROMISE

Words by
JOSEPH M. MARTIN (BMI)

Based on tunes:
SHOUT ON, PRAY ON
FOLLOWERS OF THE LAMB
SAINTS BOUND FOR HEAVEN
PROMISED LAND
Arranged by
JOSEPH M. MARTIN (BMI)

* I _____ know that my Re -

* Tune: SHOUT ON, PRAY ON, *Sacred Harp*, 2nd ed., 1850
Words: Samuel Medley, 1738-1799

* Tune: FOLLOWERS OF THE LAMB, Traditional Shaker Melody

THE SONG EVERLASTING - SATB

shout on, fol - low - ers of Em - man - u - el.

Sing on,_____ shout on, ye fol - low - ers of the

Lamb.

unis.

more smoothly

mp

* Tune: SAINTS BOUND FOR HEAVEN, *Southern Harmony,* 1835

THE SONG EVERLASTING - SATB

38

be. Grace has tru - ly set us free. Now we're

bound for Ju - bi - lee. Let us sing. Let us

sing. Now we're bound for Ju - bi - lee. Let us

sing._____ This our song shall ev - er be. Grace has

tru - ly set us free. Now we're bound for Ju - bi -

lee._____ Let us sing._____ Let us sing. Now we're

faith we_____ walk the nar - row

way, our_____ ban - ner_____ high with

praise. I am

go____ with____ me? I am bound

for the Prom - ised

Land!_____

(optional narration and congregational hymn)

NARRATOR:

And so the people began to listen to a new voice of hope. They left behind their doubts and fears and rejoiced in the graceful song of promise that was sounding in Christ's message. From over the land the people came to Him and were blessed.

His arms are outstretched still.

CONGREGATIONAL HYMN:

"I WILL ARISE AND GO TO JESUS" *(page 98)*

II. HUMILITY

NARRATOR:

Jesus stood above the city and wept. The song He had been sent to sing was heavy on His heart. His ministry among the people had angered the religious officials, and they were eager to silence this new cry of dissent that was sweeping through the land. The Passover pilgrimage to Jerusalem had brought a surge of excitement and as the day of the feast approached, Jesus and His closest followers entered the walls of the ancient city. The people were gathering for a great procession, but the music they sang was bittersweet, for it was not yet fully revealed to them the things that lay ahead. The frenzied crowds took palm branches from the trees and laid them before Jesus as He passed. They began to shout and sing, "Hosanna! Blessed is the One who comes in the name of the Lord!"

PROCESSION OF PRAISE

Words by
THEODULPH OF ORLEANS (760-821)
and **JEANETTE THRELFALL** (1821-1880)

Tune: **COMPLAINER**
Southern Harmony, 1835
Arranged by
JOSEPH M. MARTIN (BMI)

* Words: Theodulph of Orleans, 760-821
Translation: John Mason Neale, 1818-1866

King and bless-ed One!

*From Ol - i - vet they

The

fol - lowed 'mid an ex - ult - ant crowd.

vic - tor palm branch wav - ing, and chant - ing clear and

* Words: Jeanette Threlfall, 1821-1880

THE SONG EVERLASTING - SATB

48

loud. The Lord of earth and heav - en rode on in low - ly state, nor scorned that lit - tle chil - dren should on His bid - ding wait.

joice! Sing ho - san - na___ in___ the___ high - est! Sing ho -

san - na___ in___ the___ high - est! Ho - san - na

to the King!_____

NARRATOR:

As the joyous cries of "Hosanna" faded into memory, Jesus gathered to celebrate the Passover with His chosen. Kneeling as a servant, He washed His disciples feet and He taught them the meaning of true humility. There in a simple upper room they shared a meal and Jesus broke the bread and poured the wine, as was the custom. Midst the quiet chanting of Psalms and the sharing of the Passover ritual, Jesus gave them a new covenant of grace that would change the world forever. As the final tones of their evening hymn drifted into the night, they walked to Olivet and entered a garden known as Gethsemane. There, in the shadows, Jesus fell on His knees and prayed in anguish. Humbled by His obedience to the will of God, He found peace, and quietly gave Himself to His captors.

SONG OF HUMILITY

Words by
JOSEPH M. MARTIN (BMI)

Shaker Melody
Arranged by
JOSEPH M. MARTIN (BMI)

54

ne. Je - sus knelt in the gar - den, in deep hu - mil - i - ty. Je - sus wept in the gar - den, His heart in ag - o - ny. Je - sus prayed in the gar - den, be - neath the ol - ive___

Lyrics: I___ will bow and be sim - ple. I___ will bow and be free.___ I will bow and be hum - ble, bow like the wil - low___ tree. I___ will

58

bow.

bow and be sim - ple. I will bow and be

free. I will bow and be hum - ble, bow like

the wil - low tree.

Je - sus bowed in the gar - den, in dark Geth-sem - a - ne Je - sus prayed in the gar - den,_____ be-neath the ol - ive__ tree._____

mp

rit.

p

FEMALE SOLO *(opt. S.A. unis.)*

Slowly (♩= ca. 64)

pp

NARRATOR:

Stripped of His dignity and savagely beaten, the perfect "Lamb of God" stood silently before His accusers. Brutal cries of "Crucify Him" rained down from an angry mob and, for a moment, their cruelty seemed to drown out the sacred song He had come to sing. Though bowed low by violence and weighed down by a cruel cross, the heart of the Savior began to sing the music of grace. Step by step He climbed Golgotha to reclaim humanity's forgotten alleluia. Only He could proclaim the great Amen of forgiveness and restore the broken hearts of His people. Even with His final breath, He voiced a Psalm, "Father, into Thy hands I entrust my spirit."

SACRED HEAD, WONDROUS LOVE

Based on
American Folk Tunes
Arranged by
JOSEPH M. MARTIN (BMI)

* Music: American Folk Tune
Words: Paul Gerhardt, 1607-1676, tr. James W. Alexander, 1804-1859

round - ed with thorns, Thine on - ly crown; how

pale Thou art with an - guish, with sore a - buse and

scorn! How does that vis - age lan - guish which

make me Thine_ for - ev - er, and should I__ faint - ing

be._____ Lord, let me nev - er,

nev - er out - live my love to Thee. O

O sa - cred Head,_ now

* Tune: WONDROUS LOVE, American Folk Melody
Words: American Folk Hymn

THE SONG EVERLASTING - SATB

(optional narration and congregational hymn)

NARRATOR:

For three long days the world waited in silence. The heartrending music of grieving and mourning filled the earth. Deep sadness had descended upon the ones who loved Jesus. Only the lingering echoes of His assuring voice kept hope alive in their wounded spirits.

CONGREGATIONAL HYMN:

"ALAS AND DID MY SAVIOR BLEED" *(page 99)*

III. VICTORY

NARRATOR:

On the third day after the crucifixion of Jesus, the earth began to shake with anticipation. The rising sun gilded the sky with golden promise, and the garden where He had been laid, awoke to the sounds of dawn. In one great crescendo of joy, the stone rolled away from the tomb where Jesus had been laid. All creation rushed to claim its alleluia and the world broke forth in glorious song. The ancient Psalm had been fulfilled, "You have turned my mourning into joyful dancing. You have unloosed my robes of sorrow and adorned me with everlasting joy."

CHRIST IS RISEN

Words by
JOSEPH M. MARTIN (BMI)

Tunes:
NETTLETON
BEACH SPRING
Arranged by
JOSEPH M. MARTIN (BMI)

* Tune: NETTLETON, Wyeth's *Repository of Sacred Music, Part Second,* 1813

world what God has done.

Christ is ris - en!__ Christ is ris - en! Gone is death's dark mys - ter -

y. Christ is liv - ing! Christ is liv - ing!__ Love has won the vic - to -

76

Tune: BEACH SPRING, *The Sacred Harp,* 1844   THE SONG EVERLASTING - SATB

rob - in as she sings tells the sto - ry, shares the glo - ry of the

vic - t'ry of our King!

Christ is

world what God has done! Sing al - le - lu - ia! Sing al - le - lu - ia! Sing al - le - lu - ia!

NARRATOR:

With His ministry, Christ has taught us how to serve. In His humility, He has taught us how to give, and with His victory over death and sin, He has taught us how to live. For He came to give us life, a life that was more abundant and free. We have been given a new alleluia and a new voice of praise. Established in His grace, we can boldly move into the future with our hearts fixed on the things above. We can share our faith with confidence, our grateful voices united forever in the song everlasting!

commissioned for the centennial celebration of First United Methodist Church, Warrensburg, MO,
dedication of the preschool building and sanctuary restoration – December, 2008

THE SURE FOUNDATION

Words by
JOSEPH M. MARTIN (BMI)

Music by
JOSEPH M. MARTIN (BMI)
Incorporating
"How Firm a Foundation"

Come, ye thank-ful peo-ple, come.

Wake the dawn with tune-ful___ sing - ing.

This is the day that the

Lord, our God, has made.

* Words: Latin, 7th century; tr. John Mason Neale, 1818-1866

THE SONG EVERLASTING - SATB

Christ the head and cor - ner - stone; cho - sen of the

Lord and pre - cious, bind - ing all the Church in one.

Ho - ly Zi - on's help for - ev - er, and her con - fi -

* Tune: FOUNDATION, Joseph Funk's *Genuine Church Music,* 1832
Words: John Rippon's *Selection of Hymns,* 1787

THE SONG EVERLASTING - SATB

saints of the Lord, is_____ laid for your

faith in His ex - cel - lent Word! What

more can He say_____ than to you He hath

with thee. O be not dis - mayed, for _____

I am thy God, and will still give thee

aid. I'll _____ strength - en thee,

help____ thee, and cause____ thee to stand, up -

held by My righ - teous, om - nip - o - tent

hand."____

The___

Christ is now__ our sure foun - da - tion, Christ, the au - thor__

Church who on Je - sus have found - ed their

of our faith. Let us rise__ with joy - ful__ sing - ing.

faith must now rise with the dawn - ing and

94

THE SONG EVERLASTING - SATB

* Words: William B. Bradbury, 1816-1868

THE SONG EVERLASTING - SATB

(optional narration and congregational hymn)

NARRATOR:

Let us go forth with joyful singing! Let us go out with tuneful praise! Let us go living our alleluias and sharing the wondrous story of Christ in songs of everlasting praise!

CONGREGATIONAL HYMN:

"I WILL SING THE WONDROUS STORY" *(page 100)*

I WILL ARISE AND GO TO JESUS

(optional)

Words:
JOSEPH HART (1712-1768)
Refrain, anonymous

Tune:
RESTORATION
Walker's *Southern Harmony,* 1835

CONGREGATION

I will a-rise and go to Je-sus. He will em-brace me in His arms.

In the arms of my dear Sav-ior, O there are ten thou-sand charms.

Fine

1. Come, ye sin-ners, poor and need-y, weak and wound-ed,
2. Come, ye thirst-y, come, and wel-come, God's free boun-ty
3. Come, ye wea-ry, heav-y-la-den, lost and ru-ined
4. Let not con-science make you lin-ger, nor of fit-ness

sick and sore. Je-sus read-y stands to save you,
glo-ri-fy; true be-lief and true re-pen-tance,
by the fall. If you tar-ry till you're bet-ter,
fond-ly dream. All the fit-ness He re-quir-eth

D.C.

full of pit-y, love and pow'r.
ev-'ry grace that brings you nigh.
you will nev-er come at all.
is to feel your need of Him.

ALAS, AND DID MY SAVIOR BLEED

(optional)

Words:
ISAAC WATTS (1674-1748)

Tune:
CONSOLATION
Wywth's *Repository of Sacred Music,* 1813

CONGREGATION

1. A - las! and did my Sav - ior bleed and
2. Was it for crimes that I had done He
3. Well might the sun in dark - ness hide and
4. But drops of grief can ne'er re - pay the

did my Sov - 'reign die? Would He de - vote that
groaned up - on the tree? A - maz - ing pit - y,
shut his glo - ries in, when Christ, the might - y
debt of love I owe. Here, Lord, I give my -

sa - cred head for sin - ners such as I?
grace un - known, and love be - yond de - gree!
Mak - er died, for man, the crea - ture's sin.
self a - way. 'Tis all that I can do.

THE SONG EVERLASTING - SATB

I WILL SING THE WONDROUS STORY

(optional)

Words:
FRANCIS H. ROWLEY (1854-1952) (St. 1-2, 3b)
PHILIP P. BLISS (1838-1876) (St. 3a) alt.

Tune:
BEACH SPRING
The Sacred Harp, 1844

THE SONG EVERLASTING - SATB